Egypt

Shirley J. Jordan, M.S.

Publishing Credits

Content Consultant
Blane Conklin, Ph.D.

Associate Editor
Christina Hill, M.A.

Assistant Editor
Torrey Maloof

Editorial Assistants
Deborah Buchanan
Kathryn R. Kiley
Judy Tan

Editorial Director
Emily R. Smith, M.A.Ed.

Editor-in-Chief
Sharon Coan, M.S.Ed.

Editorial Manager
Gisela Lee, M.A.

Creative Director
Lee Aucoin

Cover Designer
Lesley Palmer

Designers
Deb Brown
Zac Calbert
Amy Couch
Robin Erickson
Neri Garcia

Publisher
Rachelle Cracchiolo, M.S.Ed.

Teacher Created Materials

5301 Oceanus Drive
Huntington Beach, CA 92649-1030
http://www.tcmpub.com
ISBN 978-0-7439-0428-5
© 2007 Teacher Created Materials, Inc.
Printed in Malaysia.TH001.8399

Table of Contents

Ancient Egypt

A country must learn from the past to grow and prosper. For centuries, people have looked back at the history of Egypt and learned important lessons for today. They explore the land in northern Africa where Egypt began. They find evidence of an advanced **civilization** (siv-uh-luh-ZAY-shuhn).

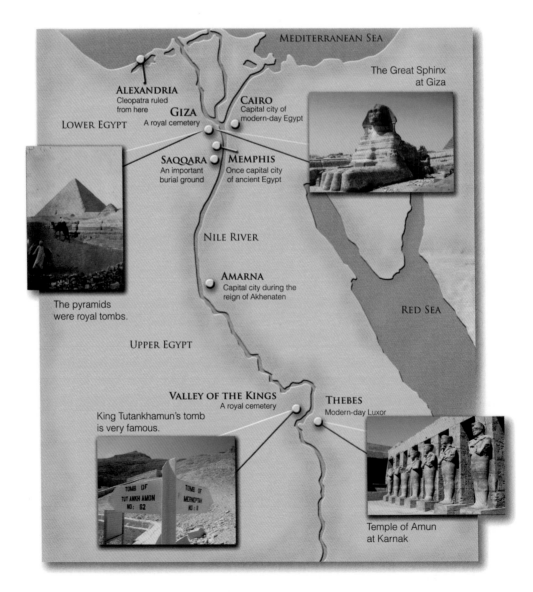

MEDITERRANEAN SEA

ALEXANDRIA
Cleopatra ruled
from here

GIZA
A royal cemetery

LOWER EGYPT

CAIRO
Capital city of
modern-day Egypt

The Great Sphinx
at Giza

SAQQARA
An important
burial ground

MEMPHIS
Once capital city
of ancient Egypt

NILE RIVER

AMARNA
Capital city during the
reign of Akhenaten

The pyramids
were royal tombs.

RED SEA

UPPER EGYPT

VALLEY OF THE KINGS
A royal cemetery

THEBES
Modern-day Luxor

King Tutankhamun's tomb
is very famous.

TOMB OF
TUT ANKH AMON
NO: 62

TOMB OF
MERNEPTAH
NO: 8

Temple of Amun
at Karnak

The Nile is the longest river in the world. The early Egyptians were the first people to live along its banks. At first, they were food gatherers who did not stay in one place. Then, they saw how important the river was to their way of life. So, they began to settle down.

During their 5,000 years of history, they learned to use the land wisely. They perfected their arts and crafts and had a gift for building. Those who came after them learned from the talent and wisdom of the ancient Egyptians.

◀ An Egyptian scribe

Keeping Records

Egypt had a written language, and some people could read and write. Those people were called scribes. They kept records in pictures and codes. The pictures and codes were discovered in modern times. They are called **hieroglyphics** (HI-ruh-glif-iks).

The Early Period

Around 5000 B.C., **nomads** began to make their homes along the Nile River in northern Africa. Nomads were normally wandering people. But, people felt safer if there were other people living near them. Their villages grew into small kingdoms. Several kingdoms ruled different parts of the river.

Each year, beginning in June, the Nile River flooded. The flooding lasted about four months. It spread wet, new soil all along the river. In most places, this wet soil stretched for about six miles (about 10 km) on either side of the river.

Grasses and reeds sprang up in the wet soil. Ducks and geese came to feed on the grasses. They built nests and laid eggs. Fish swam in the

▼ Ruins along the Nile River

shallow water at the edge of the Nile. The settlers found plenty of food and good fortune in the Nile River Valley.

The lands near where the Nile River started were called Upper Egypt. The lands where the river emptied into the Mediterranean (med-uh-tuh-RAY-nee-uhn) Sea were called Lower Egypt.

Upside-down Map

It may seem strange to us today, but Lower Egypt was to the north. This was nearer to the Mediterranean Sea. Upper Egypt was to the south because it was at the source of the Nile River.

A Kingdom United

In about 3100 B.C., there was a king of Upper Egypt named Menes (MEE-neez). His kingdom was in the south, where the river valley was very narrow. Menes knew there was more good land to the north. He wanted to join the two Egypts into one. He sent his army against the people of Lower Egypt. He united the two Egypts and become the first **pharaoh** (FAIR-o).

◄ This carving shows the **double crown** of Egypt. It was worn by the pharaohs.

The Old Kingdom and the Pyramids

Menes was followed by other pharaohs who were good leaders. Egypt was strong. The people lived well and peacefully.

After living for many years in reed huts, some settlers began to replace them with brick buildings. The brick was made from blocks of mixed mud and reeds. Brick houses were stronger and more comfortable. Soon after, the Egyptians began to build tombs called **mastabas** (MAS-tuh-buhz). This is where they buried important leaders. Mastabas were big tombs with flat tops. Inside were burial chambers and storage rooms filled with goods.

After a time, a very smart man was born. His name was Imhotep (em-HO-tep). He was probably the first person

This is a step pyramid. ▶

to find a way to build with stone. Around 2630 B.C., Imhotep created plans for the first pyramid to be built in Egypt. It was called a step pyramid. It was built to be the tomb of King Djoser (JO-suhr). The people went there to worship the spirit of the dead king.

An Unfortunate Theft

The mummy of King Djoser was buried under the pyramid Imhotep designed for him. There were six layers of rock over the body. Somehow, robbers broke into the pyramid. It was later found empty.

The Great Sphinx

The Great Sphinx (SFINKS) was built near the Pyramids at Giza. The Egyptians worshiped it as a sun god. The huge figure is almost as long as a football field. Its tallest parts are like a six-story building. The whole Sphinx is carved from one piece of **limestone**. Visitors to Egypt today never forget the Great Sphinx and the Pyramids at Giza.

The Egyptians and Mathematics

The Egyptians developed a system of numbers. They had a symbol for one and ten. They did not use the numbers two through nine. The number 25 was written in symbols as $10 + 10 + 1 + 1 + 1 + 1 + 1$.

These ancient people could multiply and divide whole numbers. They also knew how to work with fractions. They invented a system of fractions including $1/2$, $1/4$, and $1/10$. Later, they learned to use more difficult fractions, like $3/4$ and $7/10$.

When the Nile River flooded each year, it washed away land boundaries (BOUND-uh-reez). To solve this problem, the Egyptians developed a way of measuring their land by **surveying** it.

▼ Building pyramids was hard work.

Measuring accurately was also important for building monuments. To build a pyramid, huge blocks of rock had to be cut very carefully so they would fit together exactly.

During the 500-year period called the Old Kingdom, the Egyptians were very busy. They finished more than 20 important pyramids. To do this properly, they had to know about weight and volume. Written records show they also knew algebra and geometry.

▲ This document shows mathematical work by the Egyptians.

No Zero

Although the Egyptians had many symbols to help them work with numbers, they had no zero. We can only imagine today how hard it was to multiply and divide without that important placeholder.

Measuring Time

There were Egyptian **astronomers** (uh-STRAW-nuh-muhrz). They studied the planets and stars, even though they did not have telescopes. As the skies changed with the seasons, these men developed a calendar for the year. Just like ours, it was based on 365 days.

Surveying the Land

To measure land, the Egyptians tied knots in string. With the knots equally spaced apart and the string stretched out, the surveyors counted the knots and wrote down the measurements.

Religion in Everyday Life

The Egyptians had many gods. Some of them frightened people into being careful about how they acted. It was the priests who taught people about the gods. Ordinary people were not allowed inside Egyptian temples.

The moon god, Thoth, was believed to rule over all learning. Egyptians respected him for his control over numbers, weights, and measures. They also thought he could heal, and that he guided the work of doctors.

Re (sometimes called Ra) was the sun god. He was worshipped as the "father of fathers" and the "mother of mothers." The Egyptians believed that each pharaoh was a child of Re.

Amun (AH-muhn) was the name of the Egyptians' most important god. He was also called Amun-Re. That means "Amun of the Sun." His main place of worship was at Thebes (THEEBZ) in Upper Egypt.

◀ **Obelisks** (AW-buh-lisks) like this one tell the stories of the pharaohs' lives.

◀ This is a carving of Amun and Thoth.

Thoth

Many paintings and carvings of Thoth have been found. He is portrayed as a bird. The Egyptians had libraries like we do today. They believed that Thoth took care of them.

Paintings of Amun

The god Amun is painted with a human form. His headdress has two large feathers on top. In temples at Thebes, he is shown with his wife Mut.

The God Re Today

In paintings, Re is shown in human form. Usually, he has the head of a falcon. He is often shown carrying a sun disk as his symbol.

◀ This temple was in Thebes. Today, Thebes is called Luxor.

The Pharaoh

The pharaoh was the most important person in the country. Every man, woman, and child in Egypt knew of the pharaoh's power. When the pharaoh said something, the words became law. But there were no laws the pharaoh had to obey.

The people of Egypt believed their pharaoh was a god. They considered it a great honor just to kiss the dirt near his feet.

The pharaoh lived in a great palace. There were many servants who did nothing but wait on the pharaoh's family. A pharaoh usually had many wives. He chose one of them to be the "great queen." That queen's first son would have special power. When his father died, he would become pharaoh.

It was common for children within the pharaoh's family to marry each other. This kept all the power in the ruler's family. One after another, a member of the family would take the throne. A family group in power like this was a **dynasty** (DIE-nuhs-tee).

Pharaoh
Ramses II

This beautiful chair ▶
shows a pharaoh
with his great queen.

The "Great House"

The title *pharaoh* comes from two Egyptian words, *per* and *aa*. Together the two words mean "great house." So *pharaoh* came to mean "one who lives in the great house."

A Struggle for Power

When a pharaoh died, sometimes there was conflict over the throne. If the oldest son of the great queen was very young or sickly, other members of the dynasty might want to take his place. In about 1500 B.C., such a struggle involved the pharaoh's daughter, Hatshepsut (hat-SHEP-soot).

Hatshepsut ▶

The Egyptians and Death

An Egyptian man or woman wanted to live forever. Egyptians believed that a well-treated corpse would wake up some day and live again. Most Egyptian towns had a **necropolis** (nuh-CROP-uh-luhs), or a city of the dead. The streets in that part of town were lined with tombs instead of houses.

Men who knew how to take care of bodies after death were given great respect. They were called **embalmers** (im-BAWLM-uhrz).

Egyptians believed that each person had a ba, or soul. He also had a ka, an invisible twin. If the person who died was to have a proper burial, both the ba and ka had to be honored. Egyptians believed that the ba stayed in contact with the dead person's friends and all his living relatives.

The Egyptians were farmers. So, it is not surprising that they believed their souls went to a "Field of Reeds." This was their term for heaven.

They believed the spirit of the person who had died would travel to another world. There he would live with the gods and goddesses. His ka would travel back and forth between this other world and the human body.

▼ Egyptian funeral boat

Planning Ahead

Ancient Egyptians only lived to be about 40 years old. Because they wanted to be ready for death, they often began making plans before they were 20 years old.

Mourning the Dead Today

Families today show respect for the dead just as the Egyptians did. People from very rich families still have the fanciest burials. However, not everyone today expects bodies to return to life, as the ancient Egyptians did. And, we do not usually bury people's treasures in their graves.

Preparing a Mummy

In the earliest days of Egypt, tribes of nomads wandered the lands near the Nile River. The bodies of those who died still had to be taken care of. There was no ceremony attached to death at that time. But, to remove the bodies from sight and keep animals away, the remains of the person who died were buried deep in the hot desert sand.

A surprising thing happened. The buried bodies did not rot. They baked in the extreme heat of the sand so that they dried out. The person still looked much like he or she had in life.

This discovery led to **mummification**. How could you dry out a body but keep it where animals

◀ Egyptian casket

◀ Canopic jars

or floods would not uncover it? The answer was **natron** (NAY-trawn), a natural salt that dries out a corpse and leaves it quite lifelike.

There were several steps in creating a mummy. First, embalmers removed the vital organs. Only the heart remained in the body. It would be needed when the mummy returned to life. The other internal organs were placed in clay **canopic** (kuh-NO-pik) **jars**.

The body was then treated with natron and wrapped in hundreds of yards of linen. About 20 layers of wrapping were needed. Often the dead person's jewelry was placed between the layers of wrapping.

The body was then placed in a decorated casket. It was hidden in a burial chamber along with the treasures of the deceased.

The Brain

The Egyptians did not value the brain among the other human organs. Hieroglyphic pictures show embalmers removing it through the nose with a hook. Then, it was thrown away.

Examining Mummies

Today, we can learn about a mummy without unwrapping it. Scientists use X-rays. Instead of destroying the mummy, this saves it for later study.

Egyptian mummy ▶
wrapped in linen

Intruders from Other Lands

Egypt was a difficult land to protect from enemies. Its citizens lived along the long Nile River. It was very hard for an army to protect a country so long and narrow. Only the strongest and wisest of pharaohs could keep the country's borders secure. At times, people from other countries took over some of Egypt's land.

About 1730 B.C., invaders from Asia took over northern Egypt. They conquered the Nile **delta** at the Mediterranean Sea. Then, they moved farther south into the Nile River Valley. They were called the Hyksos (HIK-saws).

The Hyksos occupied large parts of Egypt for more than 100 years. The Egyptian pharaohs on the throne during that time were not strong leaders. They did not inspire their armies to push the intruders out.

◀ Egyptians conquering the Asians

Because the Hyksos stayed so long, they began to marry into Egyptian families. The Egyptians adopted some of the skills of the Hyksos, too. From these intruders, they learned to build bronze weapons and to use horses and chariots. The Hyksos also brought special cattle to the Nile Valley and new types of vegetables and fruits.

One Egyptian pharaoh, Ahmose I (AH-mohs), was finally able to drive out the Hyksos. He forced them back to Asia. However, many influences from these intruders remained part of Egyptian life.

Careful Records

One of the most surprising and important things the Hyksos did was preserve Egyptian documents. During their **reign** (RAIN), scribes recopied Egyptian texts and documents so they would not be destroyed.

A Link to the Bible

The Bible story about Joseph, who was sold into slavery by his brothers, is well-known. He later became the trusted servant of the assistant to Egypt's pharaoh. The Bible does not name that pharaoh, but some historians believe it was one of the Hyksos leaders.

The Early New Kingdom

After the Hyksos were driven out of Egypt, there was a time of peace and strong leadership. In about 1518 B.C., pharaoh Thutmose I (THUHT-mohs) brought Egypt together as a strong nation once again.

Thutmose and his great queen had four children. There were two sons and two daughters. But only one of these children lived through childhood. Her name was Hatshepsut. When she was a teenager, her father (the pharaoh) died. Egypt had never had a woman as ruler, but the throne of Egypt was empty.

Thutmose I had a son with one of his other wives. The advisors of Egypt decided that Hatshepsut would marry her young half brother, and they would rule together. The brother, Thutmose II, would be pharaoh. Hatshepsut would be his **regent** (REE-juhnt).

Thutmose II was a weak and lazy

young man. Hatshepsut was a strong woman who made most of the decisions. Thutmose II ruled for about 10 years with Hatshepsut as his regent. Then, he died. Again, Egypt's throne had no pharaoh.

Thutmose II had a son with another woman. In about 1504 B.C., the son, Thutmose III, became pharaoh. Hatshepsut was now in her twenties, and she was regent to an infant!

Thutmose III was too young to keep Hatshepsut from making the decisions about how Egypt would be ruled. After about seven years, she declared herself pharaoh and took over the throne. Young Thutmose III faded into the background at the palace and kept busy with Egypt's armies.

Hatshepsut ruled Egypt for about 22 years. When she died, Thutmose III became a strong and well-respected pharaoh. His people knew him as the "Warrior King." His reign lasted 30 more years.

Marriages Between Relatives

It was common in ancient times for brothers and sisters to marry to make the ruling family more powerful.

Marriage Partners

It was important for a young man of the pharoah's dynasty to marry the right young woman. His parents would choose her for him. In most of the world today, young people choose their own husbands and wives.

▲ A pharaoh and his two wives

◄ Thutmose III

Three Powerful Kings

In the years after Thutmose III died, three strong pharaohs ruled Egypt. They are better known in history than many leaders who lived before them.

Akhenaten (aw-kuh-NAW-tuhn) was Egypt's pharaoh from about 1379 to 1362 B.C. His wife was the beautiful Queen Nefertiti (nef-uhr-TEE-tee). Akhenaten was a religious fanatic who wanted his people to worship only one god, Aten. Akhenaten declared Aten to be the sun god. He destroyed the monuments to Egypt's other gods and drove away the priests for those gods. The people did not like his actions. Most of them did not want to abandon the many gods they believed in.

◀ Queen Nefertiti

The next pharaoh, Tutankhamun (toot-ank-AH-muhn), ruled ancient Egypt from about 1361 to 1352 B.C. He became pharaoh when he was only eight or nine years old. Tutankhamun was buried with more than 2,000 items. One of his three coffins was made from more than a ton of pure gold!

Ramses II (RAM-seez) was a pharaoh with a long reign. He is known for his years of land struggles against the invading Hittites (HIT-tites). In peacetime, Ramses built large temples throughout Egypt's cities. Sometimes he even claimed credit for the building projects of pharaohs before him.

Akhenaten's Beliefs

Some historians call Akhenaten the first world ruler to be a **monotheist** (MAW-nuh-thee-ist). That means someone who believes there is only one god. However, Akhenaten believed there were many gods. He just wanted people to worship only one.

Ramses II and the Bible

Many historians identify Ramses II as the pharaoh at the time of the Bible story of the Exodus.

The Riches of King Tut

The tomb of young King Tutankhamun was not found until 1917. That is very recent in terms of the history of Egypt. Today, great displays of his treasures are on view in museums all over the world.

▲ Statue of Ramses II

The burial ▶
mask of King
Tutankhamun

The Late Period

By 1200 B.C., many other regions had entered the Iron Age. Egypt did not have any iron ore. So, they were not able to make stronger weapons like their enemies. Attacks came from many sides. Whole Egyptian states were taken over by invaders.

By 525 B.C., the powerful Persians (PURR-zhuhnz) had driven away the other invaders. They ruled Egypt for nearly 200 years.

In 332 B.C., Alexander the Great and his Greek armies conquered Egypt and most of the known world. The Egyptians welcomed him because they disliked being ruled by the Persians. Alexander brought Greek ideas and Greek customs to all the countries he ruled. He required the people he conquered to treat him as a god.

Alexander the Great ▶

Ptolemy I

Alexander the Great died of malaria in 323 B.C. His favorite general, Ptolemy I (TAWL-uh-mee), seized Egypt as his share of Alexander's wealth.

Ptolemy brought Greek and other foreign soldiers to settle there. He developed Egypt into a great nation of industry. Ptolemy's family ruled for almost 300 years. In 51 B.C., a young woman named Cleopatra (klee-uh-PAH-truh) became queen.

By this time, the Roman Empire was expanding through all of Europe, Asia, and Africa. Egypt would soon be attacked. Cleopatra was desperate to make friends with the Romans.

An Engineering Feat

While the Persians ruled Egypt, they built a canal to the Red Sea. This opened trade with other nations.

Cleopatra's Loves

Cleopatra and the Roman emperor, Julius Caesar (SEE-zuhr), fell in love. They had a son together. When Caesar was killed, Cleopatra turned her attention to Caesar's friend, Mark Antony. They had several children together before his death.

◀ Roman emperor Julius Caesar

The End of Egypt

The glory of Egypt had been fading for many years. Finally, Cleopatra could hold off her Roman enemies no longer. Huge armies were at the very borders of Egypt.

It was the custom in ancient times for defeated rulers to commit suicide. This was a noble way to earn entry into the Field of Reeds. So, that is what Cleopatra decided to do. According to legend, she allowed herself to be bitten by a poisonous snake, which was a symbol of Egypt.

In 30 B.C., Egypt became a **province** of the mighty Roman Empire. The 3,000-year-old civilization ended.

◀ This carving of Cleopatra is on the side of an ancient Egyptian ruin.

A City for All Time

Alexander the Great built a vast city just north of the Nile's delta. He called it Alexandria. Ptolemy I named Alexandria the capital city of Egypt. Alexandria is still a leading city of the world. It is home to one of the Seven Wonders of the Ancient World, the lighthouse at Pharos (FER-aws).

◀ Sketch of the lighthouse at Pharos

Glossary

astronomers—scientists who study the stars

canopic jars—jars used in ancient Egypt to hold the internal organs of a mummified body

civilization—a society that has writing and keeps track of records

delta—a deposit of sand and soil at the mouth of a river

double crown—the crown worn by pharaohs after the unification of Upper Egypt and Lower Egypt

dynasty—a line of rulers from the same family

embalmers—workers who treat dead bodies with various chemicals

hieroglyphics—pictures or symbols representing words, syllables, or sounds; used by the ancient Egyptians instead of alphabetical writing

limestone—a hard rock formed from the bodies of sea animals and pressed down for centuries

mastabas—structures with flat roofs that served as tombs in ancient Egypt

monotheist—a person who believes there is only one god

mummification—the preservation of a body by embalming

natron—hydrated sodium carbonate used by the ancient Egyptians to dry a body

necropolis—a cemetery in an ancient city

nomads—people having no permanent homes

obelisks—tall, four-sided towers of stone covered in hieroglyphs

pharaoh—the title of kings of ancient Egypt

province—any of the outside territories controlled and ruled by ancient Rome

regent—someone who acts in the place of a king or ruler

reign—the years that a ruler is in power

surveying—determining the location, form, or boundaries of land

Index

Image Credits